ST. A
SHR

CW00401877

THE WISDOM OF SAINT IGNATIUS LOYOLA

THE
WISDOM
OF
SAINT IGNATIUS
LOYOLA

Compiled and introduced by
Margaret Silf

LION
Giftlines

Published by
Lion Publishing plc
Sandy Lane West, Oxford, England
www.lion-publishing.co.uk
ISBN 0 7459 4218 0

First edition 1999
10 9 8 7 6 5 4 3 2 1 0

Text acknowledgments

Draw me into your friendship: The Spiritual Exercises. A literal translation and a contemporary reading ('*Spiritual Exercises*'), David L. Fleming SJ, The Institute of Jesuit Sources, Saint Louis, 1996

St Ignatius' Own Story, as told to Luis Gonzalez de Camara ('*Autobiography*'), translated William J. Young SJ, Loyola University Press, Chicago, 1980

Inigo: Letters personal and spiritual ('*Letters*'), selected Michael Ivens SJ, edited and translated Joseph A. Munitiz SJ, Inigo Enterprises, 1995

The Constitutions of the Society of Jesus and their Complementary Norms ('*Constitutions*'), The Institute of Jesuit Sources, Saint Louis, 1996

Picture acknowledgments

1, 28, 29: Descent from the Cross (detail) by Spanish School (16th century), Museo de Santa Cruz, Toledo, Spain/Bridgeman Art Library, London/New York; 2: Christ, The Saviour of the World by Fernando Yanez de Almedina (d. 1560), Caylus Anticuario, Madrid, Spain/Bridgeman Art Library, London/New York; 11: The Vision of St Ignatius by Sebastien Bourdon (1616–71), Agnew & Sons, London/Bridgeman Art Library, London/New York; 17: St Andrew the Apostle (detail) by José Ribera/SuperStock Ltd; 22: Madonna and Child (detail) by Alonso Berruguete/SuperStock Ltd; 25: Ecce Homo by Bartolomé Esteban Murillo/SuperStock Ltd; 31: The Penitent Magdalen by José Ribera/SuperStock Ltd; 37: The Return of the Prodigal Son (detail) by Bartolomé Esteban Murillo/SuperStock Ltd; 43, cover: St Ignatius of Loyola, Founder of the Jesuits by Peter Paul Rubens (1577–1640), Musée de Sibiu, Romania/Giraudon/Bridgeman Art Library, London/New York; 46/47: Death of the Virgin (detail) by Pedro Machuca/SuperStock Ltd

All artwork by Vanessa Card

A catalogue record for this book is available from the British Library

Typeset in 12.5/13 Venetian 301
Printed and bound in Singapore

Contents

INTRODUCTION

We are told that a trivial incident in one part of the world can have quite unpredictable consequences in another. The laws of cause and effect reveal a vast interdependence of all created things. You are reading this book today, for example, because of a stray cannon ball fired 450 years ago during a battle between France and Spain at the fortress of Pamplona. The proud and stubborn defender of Pamplona, and the victim of that cannon ball, was Inigo Lopez, born in 1491 at Loyola in the Basque region of Northern Spain, and later to become St Ignatius Loyola.

The cannon ball that shattered Inigo's knee also triggered a radical conversion in his heart. During his prolonged and painful convalescence, he had time to reflect on the shape and meaning of his life and on what he really desired to do with it. He indulged in daydreams. Some were of worldly conquests – victories in battle and the winning of women's hearts. They gave him pleasure, but their effects quickly wore off, leaving him bored and discontented. Other daydreams were about a different kind of conquest – the visions and missions of the great saints, and the perennial human quest to strive for what is beyond the here and now. This second kind of dreaming left him feeling enlivened and inspired.

He noticed the difference and began to ponder it, embarking upon a venture into the movements of cause and effect in his own feelings, reactions and choices. Dreams built only on worldly wishes, he found, were superficial and could not sustain him. Those that touched his desire for the very best in himself had deep roots, opening up a spring of energy within him.

As he worked out these insights in practice, Ignatius explored the whole process of spiritual discovery and growth and shared his experience with a few friends, making notes in a little book that he called *The Spiritual Exercises*. These *Exercises*, which resonate remarkably with our own century's understanding of psychology, are intended to encourage us to discover for ourselves the answers to such questions as:

How can we recognize God's action in our lives?

How can we discern what is of God and what is not?

How can we live true to ourselves and make decisions in freedom?

How do we discover our deepest desires and free ourselves of the lesser attachments that obstruct them?

The *Exercises* suggests a framework of prayer which helps us to get in touch with the stirrings in our hearts and to connect the events of our own lives with those of the Christian Gospel. They develop our awareness that there is something of God to be found in everything we experience. They encourage us to respond to the positive and counteract the negative movements, and to make choices from a point of inner freedom and equilibrium. They help us to let go of what saps our spiritual energy and impedes our relationship with God, in order to seek what is more perfectly attuned to what is deepest in us.

More and more people found the *Exercises* helpful, and even life-changing, and this is still the case today. Longing to share his discoveries with others, Ignatius began to direct his energy towards mission. Together with a group of friends, he formed the Society of Jesus, a religious order which, since then, has kindled the fire of God's Spirit in the hearts of countless seekers throughout the world. The touch of God on his life now urged him out to the suffering world, where his contemplation could become effective in action and in service.

Soldier, dreamer, man of prayer and man of action, Ignatius led his companions – the Jesuits – back, through the way of prayer, into the world's struggle against despair, suffering and injustice. Today, more than at any other time since his own, his vision attracts fellow-pilgrims into the journey of the heart, providing both bread and signposts for the way.

MARGARET SILF

CALL AND
RESPONSE

THE STIRRINGS OF WONDER

One night, as he lay awake, he saw clearly the likeness of our Lady with the holy child Jesus, at the sight of which he received most abundant consolation for a considerable interval of time. He felt so great a disgust with his past life, especially with its offences of the flesh, that he thought all such images which had formerly occupied his mind were wiped out.

He began to experience great changes in his soul. Sometimes his distaste was so great that he found no relish in any of the prayers he recited. At other times everything was just the contrary, and so suddenly that he seemed to have got rid of the sadness and desolation pretty much as one removes a cloak from the shoulders of another. Here he began to marvel at these changes which he had never before experienced, saying to himself: 'What new kind of life is this that we are now beginning?'

Autobiography, 1:10, 3:21

CONTEMPLATING THE LOVE OF GOD

I put myself before Jesus Christ our Lord,
present before me on the cross. I talk to him
about how he creates because he loves and then
he is born one like us out of love, so emptying
himself as to pass from eternal life to death
here in time, even death on a cross. By his
response of love for God his Father, he dies
for my sins.

I look to myself and ask — just letting the
questions penetrate my being:
In the past, what response have I made to Christ?
How do I respond to Christ now?
What response should I make to Christ?
As I look upon Jesus as he hangs upon the
cross, I ponder whatever God may bring to
my attention.

Spiritual Exercises, 53

GOD'S GREAT DESIRE

God creates me out of love and desires nothing
more than a return of love on my part. So much
does God love me that even though I turn away
and make little response, this giver of all good
gifts continues to be my Saviour and Redeemer.

All my natural abilities and gifts, along with
the gifts of baptism and the Eucharist and the
special graces lavished upon me, are only so many
signs of how much God our Lord shares divine
life with me and wants to share ever more.

Spiritual Exercises, 234

HOW CAN I RESPOND?

I look at my world. Everything cooperates to continue to give me life and strength. I look at the whole support system of air and water, warmth and coolness, light and darkness, all the produce of the earth, all the works of human hands – everything contributes to my well-being.

I think of the people who have prayed for me and love me. The whole communion of saints has interest in my salvation and actively works to try to help me.

How can I respond to a God so good to me and surrounding me with the goodness of holy men and women and all the wonderful gifts of creation? All I can do is give thanks, wondering at God's forgiving love, which continues to give me life up to this moment.

Spiritual Exercises, 60

THE HEART OFFERS ITSELF

Eternal Lord and King of all creation, humbly
I come before you. Knowing the support of
Mary your mother, and all your saints, I am
moved by your grace to offer myself to you and
to your work. I deeply desire to be with you
in accepting all wrongs and all rejections and
all poverty, both actual and spiritual – and I
deliberately choose this, if it is for your greater
service and praise. If you, my Lord and King,
would so call and choose me, then take and
receive me into such a way of life.

Spiritual Exercises, 98

THE PILGRIM'S
JOURNEY

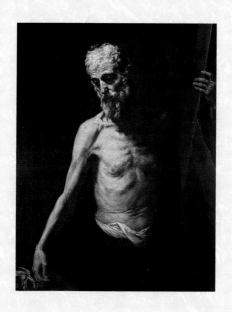

THE MIRACLE OF AWAKENING

He began to write very carefully in a book,
as he had already begun to move a little about
the house. The words of Christ he wrote in red
ink and those of our Lady in blue, on polished
and lined paper in a good hand, for he was an
excellent penman.

Part of his time he spent in writing, part
in prayer. It was his greatest consolation to
gaze upon the heavens and the stars, which
he often did, and for long stretches at a time,
because when doing so he felt within himself
a powerful urge to be serving our Lord. He
gave much time to thinking about his resolve,
desiring to be entirely well, so that he could
begin his journey.

Autobiography, 1:11

SETTING OUT

On the eve, then, of our Lady's Annunciation,
March 24th, at night, in the year 1522, he
went as secretly as possible to a poor man, and
removing his fine clothes gave them to him,
put on his desired attire, and went to kneel
before our Lady's altar.

Alternating between kneeling and standing,
with his pilgrim's staff in his hand, he thus
spent the whole night. At daybreak he left, and
to avoid being recognized, he took, not the
highway that led straight to Barcelona where he
would meet many who knew him and honoured
him, but by-ways, by which he came to a small
town called Manresa, where he decided to
spend a few days in the hospital, and to make
a few notes in his book which he carried very
carefully with him and which brought him many
consolations.

Autobiography, 2:18

'PLACE ME WITH YOUR SON'

He had made up his mind after taking orders to wait a year before saying Mass, preparing himself and praying our Lady to place him with her Son. One day, a few miles before they reached Rome, while he was praying in a church, he felt such a change in his soul, and saw so clearly that God the Father placed him with Christ his Son, that he would not dare to doubt that the Father had placed him with his Son.

Autobiography, 10:96

The most important qualities in the person who enters into these exercises are openness, generosity, and courage. Our one hope and desire is that God will place us with his Son so that in all ways we seek only to respond to that love which first created us and now wraps us round with total care and concern.

Spiritual Exercises, 5

PILGRIMAGE INTO PRAYER

I try to enter into the vision of God looking
upon our world: men and women being born
and being laid to rest… the old and the young,
the rich and the poor, the happy and the sad,
so many people aimless, despairing, hateful,
and killing, so many undernourished, sick and
dying, so many struggling with life and blind
to any meaning. With God, I can hear people
laughing and crying, some shouting and
screaming, some praying, others cursing.

The leap of divine joy: God knows the time
has come when the mystery of salvation, hidden
from the beginning of the world, will shine into
human darkness and confusion. It is as if I can
hear the Divine Persons saying: 'Let us work
the redemption of the whole human race; let
us respond to the groaning of all creation.'

I try to stay with the eyes of God, and look
upon the young girl Mary as she is greeted by
God's messenger, Gabriel.

I let myself be totally present to the scene,
hearing the nuances of the questions, seeing
the expression in the face and eyes, watching
the gestures and movements.

As I find myself immersed in the setting of
this mystery of the Incarnation, I may want just
to stay with Mary or with the eternal Word,
who has become human — for me. I may want to
speak out my joy, my thanks, my wonder. I beg
that I might come to know Jesus as a pattern
for my own living and so be able to draw close
to him.

Spiritual Exercises, 102–109

ONE COMMON SPIRIT

This Society and its members have been brought together and united in one common spirit, namely to travel abroad from one part of the world to another, among believers and unbelievers.

The spirit of the Society is to move on from one city to another in complete simplicity and modesty, and from one district to another, not to settle ourselves in one specific place.

Letter to Ferdinand I, December 1546

FINDING GOD
IN ALL THINGS

THE GIFTS OF CREATION

God loves us, creates us and wants to share life with us for ever. Our love response takes shape in our praise and honour and service of the God of our life.

All the things in this world are also created because of God's love, and they become a context of gifts, presented to us so that we can know God more easily and make a return of love more readily.

But if we abuse any of these gifts of creation, or, on the contrary, take them as the centre of our lives, we break our relationship with God and hinder our growth as loving persons.

Spiritual Exercises, 23

HELP IN ALL THINGS

I like to think that when persons go out of themselves and enter into their Creator and Lord, they enjoy continuous instruction, attention and consolation; they are aware how the fullness of our eternal God dwells in all created things, giving them being, and keeping them in existence with his infinite being and presence.

Those who love God completely find help in all things; everything supports them in their deserving efforts and in their approach to, and union with, the Creator and Lord himself through their intense love.

Letter to Francis Borgia, late 1545

IN THE IMAGE OF GOD

Look also at the people around you and realize that they are an image of the Holy Trinity. They have potential for the glory of him to whom the universe is subject. They are members of Jesus Christ, redeemed through his many pains and insults, redeemed through his blood.

Letter to the Students of the Society of Jesus in Coimbra, 7th May 1547

CONTINUAL PRAYER

A way of helping others which is very wide-ranging consists in prayers and holy desires. Study does not give you time for very long prayers, but those who make all their activities into a continual prayer, entering into them for God's service, can make up in desires for the time not spent formally praying.

Letter to the Students of the Society of Jesus in Coimbra, 7th May 1547

EVER-INCREASING GRACE

The more one binds himself to God our Lord
and shows himself more generous towards the
Divine Majesty, the more generous towards
himself and the more disposed will he be to
receive daily greater graces and spiritual gifts.

Constitutions, 282

READING THE
HEART'S COMPASS

THE MOVEMENTS OF THE HEART

There was, however, this difference…

When he was thinking of the things of the world he was filled with delight, but when afterwards he dismissed them from weariness, he was dry and dissatisfied. And when he thought of going barefoot to Jerusalem, he was consoled, not only when he entertained these thoughts, but even after dismissing them he remained cheerful.

One day his eyes were opened a little and he began to wonder at the difference and to reflect on it, learning from experience that one kind of thoughts left him sad and the other cheerful. Thus, step by step, he came to recognize the difference between the two spirits that moved him, the one being from the evil spirit, the other from God.

Autobiography, 1:8

POSITIVE AND NEGATIVE MOVEMENTS

When we are trying to follow the loving invitation of God in our life, we will find that the good spirit tends to give support, encouragement, and oftentimes even a certain delight in all our endeavours.

The evil spirit generally acts to bring about the opposite reaction. The evil spirit will subtly arouse a dissatisfaction with our own efforts, will raise up doubts and anxieties about God's love or our own response, or will upset our conscience by suggesting thoughts of pride in our attempt to lead a good life.

Spiritual Exercises, 329

RECOGNIZING THE POSITIVE

As we continue to make progress in the spiritual life, the movement of the good spirit is very delicate, gentle, and often delightful. The good spirit touches us in the way that a drop of water penetrates a sponge.

When the evil spirit tries to interrupt our progress, the movement is violent, disturbing, and confusing. The way that the evil spirit touches into our lives is more like water hitting hard upon a stone.

Spiritual Exercises, 335

COUNTERACTING THE NEGATIVE

When we find ourselves weighed down by a
certain desolation, we should not try to change
a previous decision or to come to a new decision.
The reason is that in desolation the evil spirit
is making an attempt to obstruct the good
direction of our life or to change it, and so we
would be thwarted from the gentle lead of God
and what is more conducive to our own salvation.
As a result, at a time of desolation, we hold
fast to the decision which guided us during
the time before the desolation came on us.

Spiritual Exercises, 318

So we must take great care: if the enemy is
raising us up, we ought to lower ourselves,
listing our sins and wretchedness; and if he
is casting us down and depressing us, we must
raise ourselves up in true faith and hope in the
Lord, counting the benefits we have received.

Letter to Teresa Rejadell, 18th June 1536

DRAWN BY LOVE

The fear of sin should give place to the love
and desire of all perfection and of contributing
to the greater glory and praise of Christ our
Creator and Lord.

Constitutions, 602

SURRENDER
AND CHOICE

SEEKING DIRECTION

In making a choice or in coming to a decision, only one thing is really important – to seek and to find how God is calling me at this time of my life. I know that God remains faithful in giving direction to my life. God has created me out of love, and my salvation is found in my living out a return of that love. All my choices, then, must be consistent with this given direction in my life.

Spiritual Exercises, 169

CHOOSING IN BALANCE

In everyday life, then, we must hold ourselves in balance before all created gifts in so far as we have a choice and are not bound by some responsibility. We should not fix our desires on health or sickness, wealth or poverty, success or failure, a long life or a short one. For everything has the potential of calling forth in us a more loving response to our life for ever with God. Our only desire and our one choice should be this: I want and I choose what better leads to God's deepening life in me.

Spiritual Exercises, 23

THE CONSEQUENCE OF THE CHOICE

From the moment that anyone has deliberately chosen and is utterly resolved to engage themselves on behalf of God our Lord's glory, honour and service, they are prepared to reject what is highly regarded and to welcome what is low. They are willing to make no distinction between high and low, honour or dishonour, riches or poverty, affection or dislike, welcome or rejection, in a word, the glory of the world or all the insults of our age. In future no importance can be given to those affronts in this life that remain mere words and fail to hurt a hair of our heads.

Letter to Isobel Roser, 10th November 1532

FREEDOM FULFILLED

Consider that it is no small privilege of your freedom of will to be able to return it completely in obedience to the One who gave it to you. You do not destroy it in this way; rather you bring it to perfection as you put your own wishes in line with the most sure rule of all rightness, the will of God.

Letter to the Fathers and Brothers in Portugal, 26th March 1553

A PRAYER OF SURRENDER

Take, Lord, and receive all my liberty,
my memory,
my understanding,
and my entire will –
all that I have and call my own.
You have given it all to me.
To you, Lord, I return it.
Everything is yours;
do with it what you will.
Give me only your love and your grace.
That is enough for me.

Spiritual Exercises, 234

CONTEMPLATION
IN ACTION

THE LISTENING PILGRIM

From his Manresa days the pilgrim [Ignatius] had this custom that when he ate with anyone, he never spoke at table, unless to answer briefly; but he listened to the conversation and made note of some things from which he later took occasion to speak of God. When the meal was over, that is what he did.

'Well, then, what is it you preach?'

'We do not preach,' replied the pilgrim, 'but we speak familiarly of spiritual things with a few, as one does after dinner, with those who invite us.'

Autobiography, 4:42; 7:65

THE ENERGY FOR ACTION

So, for love of our Lord, let's make a great effort in him, seeing that we owe him so much. We are more likely to reach our limit in receiving his gifts than he will be in giving them.

Letter to Inés Pascual, 6th December 1524

Consider well, then, your calling, so that on the one hand you can give great thanks to God who has given you something so great, and on the other so that you can ask God for a special favour in order to be able to respond to it. Help one another too with enthusiasm and hard work, for this is very much a necessity if you are to achieve such goals.

Letter to the Students of the Society of Jesus in Coimbra, 7th May 1547

EFFECTIVE LOVING

Love ought to show itself in deeds over and above words.

Love consists in a mutual sharing of goods.

Spiritual Exercises, 230

God's love alone is the glue which must hold together and sustain us.

Letter to Father Daniel Paeybroeck in Louvain, 24th December 1547

FRIENDS OF GOD

Friendship with the poor makes us friends of
the eternal King. Love of that poverty establishes
kings, even on this earth, and kings not of earth
but of heaven. This is evident because while the
future heavenly kingdom may be promised to
others, it is promised here and now to the poor
and those who suffer tribulation.

*Letter to Members of the Society in Padua, 6th August 1547,
from Father Polanco, by commission*

A Prayer for Blessing

Therefore I ask the One who is source of this day, like a sun of wisdom and justice, to carry through in his great generosity what he has begun in you until his work reaches fulfilment, displaying the richness of his omnipotent hand and his infinite splendour in the spiritual gifts within your minds and hearts, and through you, in those of many others.

Through him I ask you also to make yourselves open for his coming and his spiritual treasures.

Letter to the Rector and Students of the College in Coimbra, 14th January 1548